D0119401

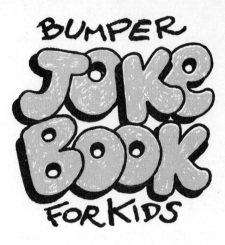

BUMPER JOKE BOOK FOR KIDS

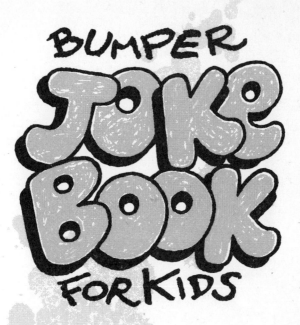

BUMPER JOKE BOOK FOR KIDS

Compiled by
Jasmine Birtles

With cartoons by
Maddocks

Michael O'Mara Books Ltd

Published in 1996 by Michael O'Mara Books Limited
9 Lion Yard, Tremadoc Road,
London SW4 7NQ

A CIP catalogue record for this book is available
from the British Library.

ISBN 1-85479-622-4

Printed in Finland by WSOY

Contents

Knock Knock jokes

Knock, knock.
Who's there?
Ann.
Ann who?
Ann amazingly good joke.

Knock, knock.
Who's there?
Isadore.
Isadore who?
Isadore on the right way round?

Knock, knock.
Who's there?
Holly.
Holly who?
Hollylujah!

Knock, knock.
Who's there?
Alf.
Alf who?
Alf way home.

Knock, knock.
Who's there?
Chester.
Chester who?
Chester drawers.

Knock, knock.
Who's there?
Cole.
Cole who?
Cole as a cucumber.

Knock, knock.
Who's there?
Eddie.
Eddie who?
Eddie-body you like.

Knock, knock.
Who's there?
Robin.
Robin who?
Robin you, so hand over your money.

Knock, knock.
Who's there?
Doctor.
Doctor Who?
That's right - where's my Tardis?

Knock, knock.
Who's there?
Isabel.
Isabel who?
Isabel necessary on a
bicycle?

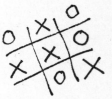

Knock, knock.
Who's there?
Lettuce.
Lettuce who?
Lettuce in and we'll tell you.

Knock, knock.
Who's there?
Evan.
Evan who?
Evan only knows!

Knock, knock.
Who's there?
Boo.
Boo who?
There's no need to cry, its only a joke!

Knock, knock.
Who's there?
Hugh.
Hugh who?
Hugh wouldn't believe it if I told you.

Knock, knock.
Who's there?
Frank.
Frank who?
Frank you very much.

Knock, knock.
Who's there?
Gary.
Gary who.
Gary on!

Knock, knock.
Who's there?
Ivan.
Ivan who?
Ivan enormous snake
in my pocket.

Knock, knock.
Who's there?
Ivor.
Ivor who?
Ivor you let me in or I'll climb
through the window.

Knock, knock.
Who's there?
Justin.
Justin who?
Justin time.

13

Knock, knock.
Who's there?
Paul.
Paul who?
Paul up a chair and I'll tell you.

Knock, knock.
Who's there?
Ray.
Ray who?
(sing) Ray drops keep falling on my head.

Knock, knock.
Who's there?
Ali.
Ali who?
Ali cat.

Knock, knock.
Who's there?
Ann.
Ann who?
Ann amazingly good joke.

Knock, knock.
Who's there?
Barbie.
Barbie who?
Barbie Q.

Knock, knock.
Who's there?
Danielle.
Danielle who?
Danielle so loud, I heard you the first time.

Knock, knock.
Who's there?
Felix.
Felix who?
Felix my lolly again I'll hit him.

Knock, knock.
Who's there?
Eva.
Eva who?
Eva had a smack in the mouth?

15

Knock, knock.
Who's there?
Gita.
Gita who?
Gita job!

Knock, knock.
Who's there?
Minnie.
Minnie who?
Minnie people want to know.

Knock, knock.
Who's there?
Liz.
Liz who?
Lizen carefully, I will say
this only once.

Knock, knock.
Who's there?
Joanna.
Joanna who?
Joanna big kiss?

Knock, knock.
Who's there?
Sigrid.
Sigrid who?
Sigrid Service.

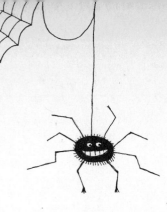

Knock, knock.
Who's there?
Summer.
Summer who?
Summer good, some
are bad.

Knock, knock.
Who's there?
Ida.
Ida who?
Ida thought you could say please.

Animal gags

What kind of tie does a pig wear?
Pigsty.

Why did the cat join the Red Cross?
Because she wanted to be a first-aid Kit.

What is a hedgehog's favourite food?
Prickled onions.

Where do milkshakes come from?
Worried cows.

Why do cats change their size?
Because they are let out at night and taken in in the morning.

Why do cows have bells?
Because their horns don't work.

What do you get if you pour boiling water down a rabbit hole?
Hot cross bunnies.

How do you stop a skunk from smelling?
Hold its nose.

What do you get if you cross a skunk with a bear?
Winnie the Pooh.

What's black, white, smelly and very noisy?
A skunk with a drumkit.

Teddy Bear Operating Manual
1. If Teddy feels hard and smooth you have not taken him out of the box. Remove at once.
2. Check to make sure that his ears are at the top of bear. If his bottom is on top you are holding him upside-down.
3. To get upside-down bear the right side up rotate him until his ears come up to the top (or you could try standing on your head).
4. Do not plug Teddy into nearest electric socket. What are you, some kind of lunatic?

5. Give Teddy a test hug. If on first squeeze bear still feels hard and smooth you are hugging the box. Can't you get rid of that stupid box?
6. If on the next hug Teddy squeals and licks your face, you have picked up the dog.
7. Don't forget to clean Teddy after every hundred thousand hugs.

How do you catch a monkey?
Hang upside down in a tree and make banana noises.

Some cows have been stolen!
It must have been a beef burglar.

What animal always goes to bed with
its shoes on?
A horse.

What did the earwig say when it fell down
the stairs?
Ear we go!

When did the fly fly?
When the spider spied 'er.

What is a crocodile's favourite game?
Snap.

'I thought I told you to take that kangeroo
to the zoo,' said the policeman.
'Well I did,' said the boy, 'And now I'm
taking it to the pictures.'

Have you put the cat out?
I didn't know it was on fire!

Why did the dog tick?
It was a watch-dog.

What goes zzub, zzub, zzub?
A bee flying backwards.

Why do bees hum?
Because they don't know the words.

What do you call a gorilla with headphones on?
Anything you like - he can't hear you.

What do you get if you sit under a cow?
A pat on the head.

Which snakes are good at maths?
Adders.

What's long and green and goes hith?
A snake with a lisp.

What do you get if you cross a snake with
a magician?
Abra da cobra.

What do polar bears have for lunch?
Ice burger.

Where do you find a tortoise with no legs?
Where you left it.

What do you call a cow that eats
your grass?
A lawn mooer.

CHOMP!
CHOMP!
CHOMP!

What's white outside, green inside and hops?
A frog sandwich.

What's green and can jump a mile a minute?
A frog with hiccups.

Where do you take a frog with bad eyesight?
To the hoptician.

What is a bear's favourite drink?
Ginger bear.

What is the best way to speak to a monster?
From a long distance.

What has a big lumpy body, twenty hairy legs and blue slimey feet?
I don't know, but it's crawling up your leg.

What did the short-sighted hedgehog say to the cactus?
Is that you, mama?

What do you get if you cross a cow, a sheep and a goat?
The milky baa kid.

Where do cows go on a saturday night?
To the moo-vies.

What goes oom, oom?
A cow walking backwards.

What is black, shiny, very dangerous and lives in trees?
A crow with a machine gun.

29

What is yellow and very dangerous?
Shark-infested custard.

What kind of tie does a pig wear?
Pigsty.

Where can you find the best
selection of cats?
In a catalogue.

What do mice do when they're
at home?
Mousework.

How do you stop your dog barking in
the hall?
Put him outside.

Why do dogs wag their tails?
Because no one will wag them for them.

What is parrot food called?
Polyfilla.

What do you get if you cross a chicken
with a cement-mixer?
A brick-layer.

Why do birds fly south in the winter?
Because it's too far to walk.

What do you call a crate of
ducks?
A box of quackers.

What do you get if you cross a sheep
with a kangaroo?
A woolly jumper.

What do you give a sick pig?
Oinkment.

Did you hear about the dog that
went to the flea circus?
It stole the show.

How do you stop a dog digging up the garden?
Take his spade away.

Why do bulldog's have such flat noses?
From chasing parked cars.

My dog has no nose.
How does he smell?
Terrible.

How do you find
your dog if he's lost in
the woods?
*Just put your ear to a tree and
listen for the bark.*

Teacher: Name four animals in the cat family.
Pupil: Mother cat, father cat and the cat twins.

What do you get if you cross a crocodile with a computer?
A computer with a lot of bytes.

What do you get if you cross a dog with a racehorse?
A dog that chases cars - and catches them!

It's raining cats and dogs.
I know, I just stepped in a poodle.

What happened when the cat ate a ball of wool?
Her kittens were all born with woolly jumpers.

Doctor doctor...

Doctor, doctor, everyone keeps ignoring me.

Next!

Doctor, doctor, I keep seeing big pink
monsters with purple spots.
Have you seen a psychiatrist?
No, just big pink monsters.

Doctor, doctor, I keep thinking I'm an
elephant.
*Don't be silly, sit down and rest your
trunk on my desk.*

Doctor, doctor, I keep thinking I'm a pair
of curtains.
Oh pull yourself together.

Doctor, doctor, everyone keeps ignoring me.
Next!

Doctor, doctor, I think I'm turning into a frog.
Well go and do it in the croakroom.

Doctor, doctor, I think I'm a dustbin.
What rubbish!

Doctor, doctor, I think I'm invisible.
Who said that?

Doctor, doctor, I've eaten too many water melons.
Oh you're just melon-choly.

Doctor, doctor, I think I'm a bumble bee.
Oh buzz off.

Doctor, doctor, I keep forgetting things.
When did this start happening?
When did what start happening?

Doctor, doctor, I've got a splitting headache.
Have you tried glueing it?

Doctor, doctor, I think I'm losing my mind.
Don't worry, you won't miss it.

Doctor, doctor, I think I'm a rubber band.
Oh snap out of it.

39

Doctor, doctor, I keep thinking I'm a telephone.
Well, take these pills and if you don't get better give me a ring.

Doctor, doctor, my wife thinks she's a clock.
Are you sure you haven't been winding her up?

Doctor, doctor, I think I'm a bread roll.
Oh stop loafing around.

Doctor, doctor, I think I'm a goat.
How long have you felt like this?
Since I was a kid.

Doctor: You need glasses.
Patient: How can you tell?
Doctor: I knew as soon as you walked through the window.

Doctor, doctor, how can I stop smoking?
Try to avoid setting fire to yourself.

Doctor, doctor, I feel like an apple.
Come over here, I won't bite you.

41

Doctor, doctor, I feel like a pack of cards.
Sit down and I'll deal with you later.

Doctor, doctor, I can't get to sleep at night.
Lie on top of the wardrobe and you'll soon drop off.

Doctor, doctor, everyone thinks I'm a liar.
I don't believe you.

Doctor, doctor, I think I'm a billiard ball.
Go to the back of the queue.

Doctor, doctor, I've swallowed the film from my camera.
I hope nothing develops.

Doctor, doctor, my head has flowers and trees growing out of it and people keep having picnics on me.
Ahhhh. I expect you've got a beauty spot.

Doctor, doctor, please come quickly, my child's just swallowed my pen.
I'll come right away, but what are you doing in the meantime?
I'm using a pencil.

Doctor, doctor, I've got carrots growing out of my ears.
How did that happen?
I don't know, I planted onions.

Doctor, doctor, I think I'm a bridge.
Now, now, what's come over you?
Two cars and a bus.

Doctor, doctor, I
think I'm a spoon.
*Stay quiet and don't
stir yourself.*

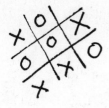

Ghoulish giggles

What do sea monsters eat?
Fish and ships.

What do you do if a monster eats your biro?
Chew your pencil instead.

What does a monster eat after he's had his teeth pulled out?
The dentist.

What do you get if you cross a ghost with a policeman?
A police in-spectre.

What would you get if a monster trod on Batman and Robin?
Flatman and Ribbon.

Why are monsters forgetful?
Because everything you say goes in one ear and out all the others.

What do you call a really nasty monster?
Sir.

What do bony people use to open doors?
Skeleton keys.

47

What skeleton was Emperor of France?
Napoleon Bone-apart.

When do ghosts play tricks on each other?
On April Ghouls' Day.

What is a devil's picket-line called?
A demon-stration.

What's a vampire's favourite drink?
A Bloody Mary.

What is Dracula's favourite pudding?
I scream.

Why do cannibals like motorway cafes?
Because they serve all sorts of drivers in them.

How does a vampire clean his house?
With a victim cleaner.

Where do vampires keep their savings?
In a blood bank.

Who's the most important member of a ghost's football team?
The ghoulie.

What does the postman take to vampires?
Fang mail.

What's the best thing to do with a green alien?
Wait until he's ripe.

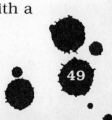

What do vegetarian cannibals eat?
Swedes.

What's a vampire's favourite fruit?
Necktarines.

What do vampires play poker for?
High stakes.

Why did the skeleton run up the tree?
Because a dog was after his bones.

What do cannibals eat at parties?
Buttered host.

What happens when aliens hold a beauty contest?
Nobody wins.

Did you hear about the cannibal who had bad indigestion?
He ate someone who disagreed with him.

What does a polite monster say?
Pleased to eat you.

What do you call a clever monster?
Frank Einstein.

How did Frankenstein eat his food so quickly?
He bolted it down.

What do ghosts eat for dinner?
Ghoulash.

What is a vampire's favourite breakfast cereal?
Ready neck.

What kind of dog did Count Dracula get?
A blood-hound.

What do monsters like eating?
Baked beings on toast.

What do sea monsters eat?
Fish and ships.

What's the difference between a monster and a biscuit?
You can't dip a monster into your milk.

Why are vampires so stupid?
Because they're suckers.

What does a polite vampire say after he has bitten you?
Fangs very much.

What kind of jewels do monsters wear?
Tombstones.

Why did the big hairy monster buy two
tickets at the zoo?
One to get in and one to get out.

What do devils drink?
Demonade.

Did you hear about the toothless
vampire?
He could give you a nasty suck.

How does a vampire cross the ocean?
On a blood vessel.

What is a vampire's favourite food?
Scream of tomato.

What is a monster's favourite game?
Swallow my leader.

Terrific teasers

Which vegetable is strong and green?
A muscle sprout.

What do fairy children do after school?
Their gnome work.

What has a bottom at the top of it?
A leg.

What do you call a wicked old woman
who lives by the sea?
A sandwich.

Have you heard about the man who
wanted to dance and cut his
toenails at the same time?
He invented the sword dance.

What do you get if you cross the
ocean with a dinosaur?
Wet.

What do you call a wizard from outer
space?
A flying sorcerer.

Why are policemen strong?
Because they can hold up traffic.

What did the traffic light say to the car?
Don't look now, I'm changing.

Where do elves go to get fit?
Elf farms.

Where do astronauts leave their
space ships?
At parking meteors.

What do you give a sick bird?
Tweetment.

Little Miss Muffet
Sat on a tuffet
Eating her Irish stew
Down came a spider
And sat down beside her
So she went and ate all that too.

What's 300 feet high and wobbly?
The trifle tower.

What's red and green?
A tomato working part-time as a cucumber.

What is yellow, brown and hairy?
Cheese on toast dropped on the carpet.

Which vegetable is strong and green?
A muscle sprout.

Mummy, mummy I can't work on an
empty stomach.
Well try the table then.

What do you call a witch's motorbike?
A brrrrooom stick.

Why did the granny have roller boots
fitted to her rocking chair?
She wanted to rock and roll.

What did the big telephone say to the
little telephone?
You're too young to be engaged.

What did the big chimney say to the
little chimney?
You're too young to smoke.

She stood on the bridge at midnight
Her lips were all a-quiver
She gave a cough
Her leg dropped off
And floated down the river.

What do you call a friendly and
handsome wizard?
A failure.

When is a door not a door?
When it is ajar.

Why couldn't the bicycle stand up?
Because it was tyred.

Who invented the first plane that
could not fly?
The wrong brothers.

What has one horn and gives milk?
A milk lorry.

Why are babies so jolly?
Because they are full of nappiness.

If a crocodile makes a pair of shoes,
what do you make from banana
skins?
Slippers.

How do you start a teddy bear race?
'Ready, teddy, go...'

Why did the banana go out with
the prune?
Because he couldn't find a date.

Little Miss Muffet
Sat on a tuffet
Eating chicken and chips
Her sister who's hateful
Nicked half a plateful
And strolled away licking her lips.

What lives under the sea and carries a lot of people?
An octobus.

Do babies go on safari?
Not safari as I know.

Who gets the sack every time he goes to work?
The postman.

Why did the boy throw his clock out
of the window?
To see time fly.

Mummy, mummy, what's a werewolf?
Be quiet Bill and comb your face.

What do traffic wardens have in their
sandwiches?
Traffic jam.

Why did the biscuit cry?
*Because his mother had been
a wafer so long.*

A little girl's Gran said to her, 'Eat your greens, or you won't grow up into a beautiful lady.'
The little girl asked her, 'Didn't you eat your greens then?'

What race is never run?
A swimming race.

Where does Tarzan buy his clothes?
A jungle sale.

What cake is dangerous?
Attila the bun.

What happened when Moses had a
headache?
God gave him some tablets.

What kind of children live on the sea?
Buoys and gulls.

How do you help deaf oranges?
Give them a lemon aid.

Why did the dinosaur cross the road?
Because chickens hadn't been invented.

When is a car not a car?
When it has turned into a lay-by.

What did the Martian say to the petrol pump?
Take your finger out of your ear when I'm talking to you.

Elephants

Why do elephants lie down?
They can't lie up.

What's the best way to catch an elephant?
Act like a nut and he'll follow you anywhere.

What is big and grey and protects you from the rain?
An umbrellaphant.

Why do elephants lie down?
They can't lie up.

How do you get down from an elephant?
You don't, you get down from a duck.

QUACK!

Why did the elephant paint his head yellow?
To see if blondes have more fun.

What is big, grey and loves curry?
An Indian elephant.

Which side of an elephant has the most skin?
The outside.

What's big, wrinkled and green?
An unripe elephant.

What did the grape say when the elephant trod on it?
Nothing, he just let out a little wine.

Why do elephants paint their toenails red?
So that they can hang upside down in cherry trees.
Have you ever seen one?
No.
You see, it works!

Two elephants wanted to go swimming at the same time but they couldn't because they only had one pair of trunks between them.

How many giraffes can you get in a mini?
Four - two in the front and two in the back.

How many elephants can you get in a mini?
None, the giraffes are in it.

73

What's big, grey, very heavy and
wears glass slippers?
Cinderellaphant.

Why do elephants have trunks?
Because they'd look silly with handbags.

What's grey, has four legs and a
trunk?
A mouse going on holiday.

Why did the elephant wear sunglasses on
the beach?
Because he didn't want to be recognized.

Where does an elephant go on holiday?
Tuscany.

Why are elephants big, grey and wrinkly?
Because if they were small, round and white they would be aspirins.

What should you do
if an elephant
charges?
Pay and run.

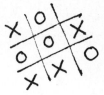

How do you know if an elephant has been in your fridge?
There are footprints in the butter.

Why do elephants paint their feet yellow?
So that they can float in custard.

Why did the elephant cross the road?
Because it was the chicken's day off.

Why do elephants have wrinkles?
Have you ever tried ironing one?

What do you get if you cross an
elephant with a loaf of bread?
A sandwich that will never forget.

Why don't elephants like penguins?
They can't get the wrappers off.

What's big, heavy and grey and has
sixteen wheels?
An elephant on roller-skates.

What do elephants sing at Christmas?
Jungle bells.

What do you get if you cross an
elephant with a kangaroo?
Great big holes all over Australia.

What's the biggest ant in the world?
An eleph-ant.

What happened to the elephant
when he drank too much?
He got trunk.

What do you call the stupidest
elephant in the world?
Dumbo.

What do you get if an elephant sits on
your best friend?
A flat mate.

What do you get if an elephant sits
on your piano?
A flat note.

How do elephants get power?
With ele-tricity.

Why do elephants paint
their ears green and their
trunks red?
*So that they can hide in
rhubarb patches.*

Why do elephants live in the jungle?
Because they're too big to live in a house.

How do you get an elephant
into a car.
Open the door.

Why do elephants have big ears?
Because Noddy wouldn't pay the ransom.

What do you call an elephant in a
phone box?
Stuck.

What's big, red and hides behind a bush?
An embarrassed elephant.

Teacher: This homework's in your father's writing.

Pupil: Yes, sir, I used his pen.

Teacher: If you had 20 pence and you asked your granny for another 20 pence and your grandpa for 30 pence, what would you have?
Pupil: 20 pence, sir.
Teacher: You don't know your maths.
Pupil: You don't know my grandparents.

Teacher: If you don't pay attention I'll give you a piece of my mind.
Pupil: Are you sure you can spare it, miss?

Teacher: What time of the day was Adam born?
Pupil: In the afternoon.
Teacher: Why do you say that?
Pupil: Because he was born just before Eve.

Teacher: How did you miss school yesterday?
Pupil: I didn't miss it one little bit, sir.

Teacher: Spell 'hungry horse'.
Pupil: M.T.G.G.

Teacher: You have your shoes on the wrong feet.
Pupil: They're the only feet I have, miss.

Teacher: I wish you'd pay a little attention.
Pupil: I'm paying as little attention as I can miss.

Teacher: Give me a sentence with the word 'indisposition' in it.
Pupil: I always play centre forward because I like playing in dis position.

Pupil: Please miss, would you punish me for something I didn't do?
Teacher: No, of course not.
Pupil: Oh good because I didn't do my homework.

Teacher: Who wrote, 'To a Mouse'?
Pupil: I don't know, but I shouldn't think he got an answer.

Teacher: This homework's in your father's writing.
Pupil: Yes, sir, I used his pen.

Teacher: John, what was the name of the first woman on earth?
Pupil: Give me a clue, miss.
Teacher: Think of an apple.
Pupil: Granny Smith, miss.

Teacher: If I have 20 chips in one hand, and 10 in the other, what do I have?
Pupil: Greasy hands.

Teacher: Stop showing off! Do you think you are the teacher of this class?
Pupil: No sir.
Teacher: So stop acting like a fool.

Teacher: You should have been here at 9 o'clock.
Pupil: Why, what happened?

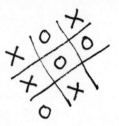

Teacher: How were your exam questions?
Pupil: They were easy but I had trouble with the answers.

Teacher: What do you know about the Dead Sea?
Pupil: I didn't even know it was ill, miss.

Teacher: I hope I didn't see you looking at Bill's work.
Pupil: I hope you didn't either, sir.

Teacher: If you had 50p in one trouser pocket and 75p in the other what would you have?
Pupil: Someone else's trousers on, miss.

Teacher: Name two days of the week beginning with 'T'.
Pupil: Today and tomorrow.

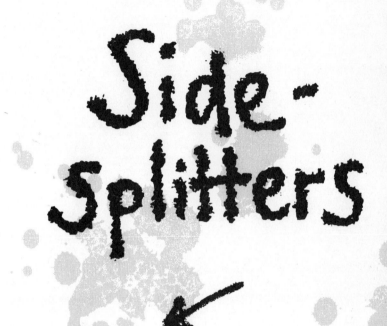

Side-splitters

What did the policeman say to his tummy? You're under a vest.

Why did the cleaning lady stop working?
Because she found that grime doesn't pay.

What is higher than a general?
His hat.

How do you make antifreeze?
Hide all her jumpers.

What sort of lights did Noah's Ark have?
Floodlights.

Why is it difficult to keep a secret on a cold day?
Because your teeth chatter.

Why didn't anyone take the school bus to school?
Because it wouldn't fit through the door.

Why was the doctor working on the motorway?
It needed by-pass surgery.

What is big, hairy and flies to New York faster than sound?
King Kongcorde.

What do you get in newspapers on
Fridays?
Fish and chips.

Why were the firemen called to the
flowerbed?
Because it was ablaze with colour.

Why did the baby biro cry?
*Because it's mother was doing a long
sentence.*

Why should you never put the letter
'M' in the fridge?
Because it turns 'ice' into 'mice'.

91

Why are you so angry?
Oh it's all the rage now.

Why do witches get good bargains?
Because they like to haggle.

Mummy, mummy, do you notice any change in me?
No dear, why should I?
I've just swallowed 5p.

When is a boat like a fall of snow?
When it is adrift.

Where does Dracula get all his jokes?
From his crypt writer.

What do you call high-rise flats for pigs?
Sty scrapers.

What happened to the robber who
pinched a bar of soap?
He made a clean getaway.

What did the astronaut see in his
frying pan?
An unidentified frying object.

How did the dentist become a brain
surgeon?
His drill slipped.

Why is a bald man's head like Alaska?
It's a great white bear place.

How do you get a baby astronaut to
sleep?
You rock-et.

What do you do if you find a blue apple?
Try to cheer it up.

Why did the bank robber have
a bath?
*So that he could have a clean
getaway.*

What kind of clothes did people wear
during the Great Fire of London?
Blazers.

What do policemen have for lunch?
Truncheon meat sandwiches.

What did one eye say to the other?
Between us is something that smells.

Mummy, mummy, I don't want to go
to America.
Be quiet and keep swimming.

What do cats strive for?
Purrfection.

Who wrote the book on
seasickness?
Eva Lott.

Why do wizards drink tea?
Because sorcerers need cuppas.

What's an Ig?
An Eskimo's house without a toilet.

My brother's built upside down. His nose runs and his feet smell.

Why shouldn't you tell jokes when you are ice-skating?
Because the ice might crack up.

Your stomach's too fat, you'll have to diet.
All right, but what colour?

Mary had a little lamb
He had a touch of colic
She gave him brandy twice a day
And now he's alcoholic!

Mummy, mummy, do I have to wash my
hands before playing the piano?
Not if you only play the black notes.

Where does a general keep his armies?
Up his sleevies.

What did the policeman say to his
tummy?
You're under a vest.

The Loch Ness monster was swimming around one day when suddenly he was attacked by six giant squid. He killed them, one by one, and then swam with them up to the surface. There he met an old fisherman friend of his. 'Hey, Jock,' he said, 'here's the six squid I owe you.'

Where does your sister live?
Alaska.
Don't worry I'll ask her myself.

What kind of bow is impossible
to tie?
A rainbow.

Did you hear about the ugly baby?
It was so frightful its parents ran away from home.

What do you call a sorceress who asks for lifts in cars?
A witch hiker.

What type of fairy eats the fastest?
A goblin.

Why are you dancing with that jar of jam?
It says 'Twist to Open'.

What do you call a robbery in Beijing?
A Chinese take-away.

What do elves eat for tea?
Fairy cakes.

What's Chinese and deadly
dangerous?
Chop Sueyside.

What gets wetter as it dries?
A towel.

How do you make an apple puff?
Chase it round the garden.

How do you make a band-stand?
Hide all their chairs.

What nuts can be found in space?
Astronuts.

Why don't witches wear
a flat hat?
*Because there's no point
in it.*

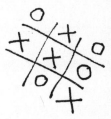

How do you know if the teacher loves
you?
She puts kisses by your sums.

What jumps from cake to cake and tastes
of almonds?
Tarzipan.

Two boys were fighting in the playground. The teacher separated them and told them off.
'You must learn to give and take,' she said.
'But we do miss,' said one boy. 'I gave John a thump and he took my apple.'

Wacky wildlife

←

Who tells chicken jokes?
Comedi-hens.

What goes krab, krab?
A dog barking into the mirror.

What do you get if you cross a cat
with a parrot?
A carrot.

What game do cows play at parties?
Moosical chairs.

What is a cat's favourite TV programme?
Miami Mice.

How do sheep keep warm when it's cold?
Central bleating.

Why don't cows make good dancers?
Because they have two left feet.

Why did the dachsund
bite the woman's ankle?
*Because he was short
and he couldn't reach
any higher.*

What did one flea say to another after a
night out?
'Shall we walk home or take a dog?'

Where do lions go if they lose their tails?
Retail shops.

What is a dog's favourite food?
Anything that's on your plate.

Has your cat ever had fleas?
No, just kittens.

When is the best time to take a
Rottweiler for a walk?
Any time he wants to go.

A man was eating fish and chips in the street when a woman walked past with a small dog. The dog started yapping at the man's food.
'Can I throw him a bit?' asked the man.
'Of course,' said the lady.
So the man picked up the dog and threw it over a wall.

What's the difference between a buffalo and a bison?
You can't wash your hands in a buffalo.

When is the best time to buy budgies?
When they're going cheap.

Why couldn't the butterfly go to the dance?
Because it was a moth-ball.

What noise does a cat make going down the M1?
Miaoooooooooooooooooooooooow.

What kind of ears do engines have?
Engineers.

Who tells chicken jokes?
Comedi-hens.

How do you find out where a flea has bitten you?
Start from scratch.

What did the bull say to the cow?
When I fall in love, it will be for heifer.

Why is it dangerous to play cards in
the jungle?
Because of all the cheetahs.

What do you call a nervous insect?
Jitterbug.

What do you call a penguin in the desert?
Lost.

What animals need oiling?
Mice, because they squeak.

When should a mouse carry
an umbrella?
When it's raining cats and dogs.

Why did the termite eat a sofa
and two chairs?
It had a suite tooth.

What goes hum-choo, hum-choo?
A bee with a cold.

What has six legs, bites and
talks in code?
A morse-quito.

What is the biggest moth?
A mam-moth.

Why did the butterfly?
Because it saw the milk-float.

110

What would you do with a sick wasp?
Take it to waspital.

What animal is best at cricket?
A bat.

Why can't you fool a snake?
He has no leg to pull.

What should you do if you find a
snake in your bed?
Sleep in the wardrobe.

How does an octopus go to war?
Well-armed.

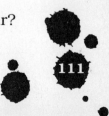

Who snatched a baby octopus?
Squidnappers.

What happens when a frog's car
breaks down?
It gets toad away.

What is a slug?
A snail with a housing problem.

Which brand of petrol do snails prefer?
Shell.

What do you call a dog with a bunch
of daisies on its head?
A collie-flower.

Why are gorillas big and hairy?
So you can tell them apart from gooseberries.

 Where does a huge
rhinocerous sleep?
Anywhere it wants to.

Which monkeys are white and fluffy?
Meringue-utangs.

What do you get if you cross a cow
with a camel?
Lumpy milkshakes.

What do you get if you cross a skunk with
an astronaut?
An animal that stinks to high heaven.

What smells worse than a pig in a sty?
Two pigs in a sty.

How do you take a pig to hospital?
By hambulance.

What does a cat have for breakfast?
Mice crispies.

What do you get if you cross a snake with
a Lego set?
A boa constructor.

Where do spiders live?
Crawley.

What do you get if you give a chicken
whisky?
Scotch eggs.

114

What kind of bird lays electric eggs?
A battery hen.

How do you catch a wild duck?
Buy a tame one and annoy it.

What is the best way to
communicate with a fish?
Drop it a line.

Which part of a fish weighs the most?
Its scales.

What is a horse's favourite game?
Stable tennis.

How do you stop a mole digging in your
garden?
Hide his spade.

Why was the cat so small?
It only drank condensed milk.

What do you call a dog with no legs?
*It doesn't matter what you call him,
he still won't come.*

What do you call a pig with no clothes on?
Streaky bacon.

What do cats read in the mornings?
Mewspapers.

What has fifty legs but can't walk?
Half a centipede.

Christmas
Crackers

↙

What exams do snowmen take?
Snow levels.

What do you get if you cross a snowman
with a crocodile?
Frostbite.

What do angry mice send each other
at Christmas?
Cross mouse cards.

What do you call a box of ducks in
the winter?
Christmas quackers.

Why does Father Christmas like to work
in the garden?
Because he likes to hoe, hoe, hoe.

What exams do snowmen take?
Snow levels.

How many legs does a reindeer have?
Six - forelegs and two back legs.

How many chimneys
does Santa have to
climb down each
Christmas?
Stacks.

What do you call a reindeer with one eye?
I've no eye-deer.

What is the wettest sort of animal?
A reindeer.

How do snowmen slim?
They stand out in the rain.

What do snowmen call their babies?
Chill-dren.

Why does Santa always climb down
chimneys?
Because it soots him.

Where do snowmen go to dance?
Snowballs.

Father Christmas have any qualifications?
Yes, three ho, ho, ho levels.

What nationality is Father
Christmas?
North Polish.

What is Mrs Santa's real name?
Mary Christmas.

What's white, furry and smells of
peppermint?
A polo bear.

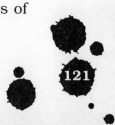

What do you call a tug-of-war on
24th December?
Christmas Heave.

What do people sing at a
snowman's birthday party?
'Freeze a Jolly Good Fellow.'

What do the British call
Christmas?
Yule Britannia.

What stays hot in a snowman's house?
Mustard.

Why is a Christmas pudding like the sea?
Because it's full of currants.

Funny business

↙

Why did the apple turnover?
Because it saw the swiss roll.

What do you call a Scottish cloakroom
attendant?
Angus MaCoatup.

A boy was seen by his father burying
his radio in the garden.'What are you
doing, son?' he asked.
*'I'm burying my radio - the batteries
are dead.'*

Why did the bald man paint rabbits
on his head?
*Because from a distance they
looked like hares.*

What is soft and yellow and goes
round and round?
A long-playing omelette.

Did you hear the one about the
three eggs?
No?
Two bad.

Have you heard about the man who was
sitting on a park bench with a carrot in
each ear?
A woman came up to him and said,
'Excuse me, but you've got a carrot in
each ear.'
He said, 'I'm sorry, I can't hear you - I've
got a carrot stuck in each ear.'

Mummy, mummy, can I have a glass of water?
You've had ten already.
I know but my bedroom's on fire.

Why should you never tell secrets in the greengrocers?
Because potatoes have eyes and beanstalk.

Did you hear about the cowboy who never had any money?
His name was Skint Eastwood.

127

What happened to the naughty witch
schoolgirl?
She was ex-spelled.

What do you call a train loaded with
toffee?
A chew chew train.

Why did the apple turnover?
Because it saw the swiss roll.

What's yellow and goes click?
A ballpoint banana.

What is always coming but never
arrives?
Tomorrow.

Why did the peanut go to the police?
He'd been a-salted.

What do you call a mushroom that
gives you a great day out?
A fungi to be with.

How do you make a sausage roll?
Push it down the hill.

Why did the egg go to the jungle?
Because it was an eggsplorer.

Have you heard about the boy who
took a pencil to bed?
*He said it was so he could draw the
curtains.*

What do Eskimos call
their money?
Ice lolly.

What's small and wobbly and sits in
a pram?
A jelly baby.

What do you call a one-eyed dinosaur?
A D'youthinkesaurus.

Mummy, mummy, can I go out
to play?
With your new suit?
No, with Mark next door.

What do you call two rows of cabbages?
A dual cabbage-way.

What's green and goes boing, boing,
boing?
A spring cabbage.

Why did the witch put her broom in
the washing machine?
She wanted to have a clean sweep.

130

I'd like to have your picture
It would look very nice
I'd put it in the cellar
To frighten all the mice.

What is the fastest vegetable?
A runner bean.

What game does a Tyrannosaurus
Rex like playing with humans?
Squash.

What do you call a flying policeman?
A heli-copper.

Why was the Egyptian girl worried?
Because her daddy was a mummy.

Why can't I tell you the joke about
the bed?
Because it hasn't been made yet.

What did the bell say when it fell in
the water?
I'm wringing wet.

What's wrong with a man who has
jelly in one ear and sponge cake in
the other?
He's a trifle deaf.

Have you heard about the eskimo who found a way to keep the roof on his house?
Iglood it.

What kind of thief steals meat?
A hamburglar.

What's the best thing to put in a cake?
Your teeth.

Mummy, mummy, I'm homesick.
But this is your home.
I know, and I'm sick of it.

What goes ha, ha, ha, plop?
A dinosaur laughing his head off.

133

There was a young lady from Surrey
Who cooked up a large pot of curry
She ate the whole lot
Straight from the pot
And ran to the tap in a hurry.

What is square and green?
A lemon in disguise.

Why did the tomato go red?
Because she saw the salad dressing.

Which dinosaur knows more words
than any other?
A thesaurus.

134

Did you hear about the thieves who stole a van full of wigs?
Police are combing the area.

Waiter Waiter...

Waiter, waiter, what's this fly doing in my soup?
I think it's the backstroke madam.

Waiter, waiter, this soup tastes funny.
Then why aren't you laughing?

Waiter, waiter, I'm in a hurry - will
my pancake be long?
No, sir, it will be round.

Waiter, waiter, what's this fly doing
in my soup?
I think it's the backstroke, madam.

Waiter, waiter, there's a small slug in
my salad.
Sorry, sir, I'll get you a bigger one.

139

Waiter, waiter, do you have frog's legs?
No, madam, I've always walked like this.

Waiter, waiter, your sleeve is in
my soup.
Oh, there's no arm in it.

Waiter, waiter, this egg is
bad.
*Don't blame me, madam,
I only laid the table.*

Waiter, waiter, there's a fly in my soup.
What do you expect for 50p, sir, a beetle?

Waiter, waiter, this soup's full of
toadstools.
*Yes, sir, there wasn't mushroom for
anything else.*

Waiter, waiter, there's a button on
my plate.
*It must have fallen off the jacket
potato, sir.*

Waiter, waiter, there's a fly in my soup.
Not fussy what they eat are they, sir?

Waiter, waiter, how
did this bluebottle get
in my soup?
*I expect it just flew in,
madam.*

Waiter, waiter, this chicken's only got
one leg.
Perhaps it's been in a fight, sir.
In that case bring me the winner.

Waiter, waiter, this coffee tastes like earth!
*I'm not surprised, it was ground this
morning.*

Waiter, waiter, bring me something to eat
and make it snappy.
Will a crocodile sandwich do, sir?

Even more Knock, knock jokes

Knock, knock.
Who's there?
Dish.
Dish who?
Dish ish a shtick-up!

Knock, knock.
Who's there?
Ben and Anna.
Ben and Anna who?
Ben and Anna split.

Knock, knock.
Who's there?
Eileen.
Eileen who?
Eileen against the door.

Knock, knock.
Who's there?
Avenue.
Avenue who?
Avenue learnt my name yet?

Knock, knock.
Who's there?
Bull.
Bull who?
Bull the chain.

Knock, knock.
Who's there?
Canoe.
Canoe who?
Canoe lend me a fiver?

Knock, knock.
Who's there?
Cook.
Cook who?
That's the first one I've heard this year.

Knock, knock.
Who's there?
Diesel.
Diesel who?
Diesel make you feel better.

Knock, knock.
Who's there?
Dish.
Dish who?
Dish ish a shtick-up!

Knock, knock.
Who's there?
Dozen.
Dozen who?
Dozen anyone know my name?

Knock, knock.
Who's there?
Haydn.
Haydn who?
Haydn in the bushes.

Knock, knock.
Who's there?
Musketeer.
Musketeer who?
Musketeer a doorbell - I'm tired of knocking.

Knock, knock.
Who's there?
Oil.
Oil who?
Oil be seeing you.

Knock, knock.
Who's there?
Snow.
Snow who?
Snow good asking me.

Knock, knock.
Who's there?
Pizza.
Pizza who?
Pizza the action.

Knock, knock.
Who's there?
You.
You who?
Did you call?

148

Knock, knock.
Who's there?
Thistle.
Thistle who?
Thistle be the last time I knock.

Knock, knock.
Who's there?
Felix.
Felix who?
Felixtremely cold.

Knock, knock.
Who's there?
Annette.
Annette who?
Annette curtain looks good in the window.

Knock, knock.
Who's there?
Frances.
Frances who?
Frances on the other side of the Channel.

Knock, knock.
Who's there?
Wayne.
Wayne who?
(sing) Wayne in a manger, no
crib for a bed.

Knock, knock.
Who's there?
Smee.
Smee who?
Smee, your friend.

Knock, knock.
Who's there?
A small boy who couldn't reach the doorbell.

150

Knock, knock.
Who's there?
Juan.
Juan who?
Juance upon a time there
were three bears...

Knock, knock.
Who's there?
Avon calling - your bell's broken.

Knock, knock.
Who's there?
Colin.
Colin who?
Colin and see me next time you're
passing.

Knock, knock.
Who's there?
Albert.
Albert who?
Albert you'll never guess.

Knock, knock.
Who's there?
May.
May who?
(sing) Maybe it's because I'm
a Londoner...

151

Knock, knock.
Who's there?
Barbara.
Barbara who?
(sing) Barbara black sheep have you
any wool...

Knock, knock.
Who's there?
Olive.
Olive who?
Olive in this house -
what are you doing
here?

Knock, knock.
Who's there?
Luke.
Luke who?
Luke through the peep-hole and
you'll see.

Knock, knock.
Who's there?
Alex.
Alex who?
Alex plain later if you let me in.

Knock, knock.
Who's there?
Una.
Una who?
Yes, Una who.

Knock, knock.
Who's there?
Yvonne.
Yvonne who?
Yvonne to know what you are doing.

153

Zany names

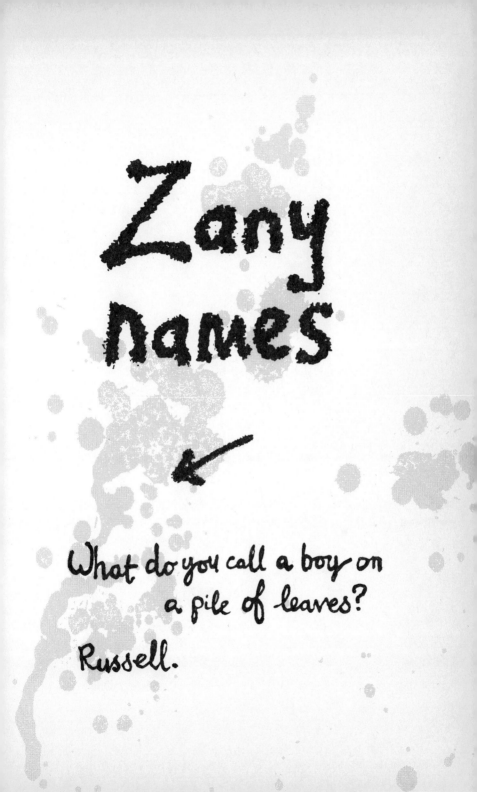

What do you call a boy on
a pile of leaves?

Russell.

What do you call a boy with a rabbit
hutch on his head?
Warren.

Who is skinny, well-dressed and
rules the waves?
The Princess of Whales.

What do you call an Irishman who's
been dead for 2,000 years?
Peat.

What do you call a boy with one foot in
the door?
Justin.

Who was the first underwater spy?
James Pond.

What do you call a girl who thinks she's a station?
Victoria.

What do you call a boy who gets up your nose?
Vic.

What do you call a boy on a pile of leaves?
Russell.

Which dinosaur wrote *Jane Eyre*?
Charlotte Brontesaurus.

What do you call a lady in the distance?
Dot.

What do you call a singing vegetable?
Tina Turnip.

What detective writer was white and lacy?
Sir Arthur Conan Doily.

What do you call a man who's
always around when you want him?
Andy.

What do you call a man with a car
on his head?
Jack.

What do you call a man who steals a lot?
Robin.

What do you call a girl with one leg?
Eileen.

159

What do you call a woman who sets fire to her bills?
Bernadette.

What do you call a boy with a seagull on his head?
Cliff.

What do you call a man with numbers down his front?
Bill.

What Elizabethan explorer could stop bikes?
Sir Frances Brake.

What do you call a boy with a
wooden head?
Edward.

What do you call a man who can sing and
drink lemonade at the same time?
A pop singer.

What do you call a girl with only one trouser leg?
Jean.

What to you call a man with a blue light on his head?
Nick.

What do you call a man with a number plate on his head?
Reg.

What do you call a man with a plastic coat?
Mac.

What do you call a girl with a frog on her head?
Lily.

What do you call a man with a spade on his head?
Doug.

What do you call a man without a spade on his head?
Douglas.

What's green and holds up
stagecoaches?
Dick Gherkin.

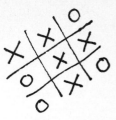

What do you call a girl
with one foot either
side of the river?
Bridget.

What do you call a camel with three
humps?
Humphrey.

What do you call a woman with two toilets?
Lou Lou.

What do you call a girl who gambles?
Betty.

What do you call a girl standing between two goalposts?
Annette.